D0106231

THE
ILLUSION

*Tony Kushner
freely adapted from
Pierre Corneille's*
*L'ILLUSION
COMIQUE*

BROADWAY PLAY PUBLISHING INC
224 E 62nd St, NY, NY 10065
www.broadwayplaypub.com
info@broadwayplaypub.com

THE ILLUSION
© Copyright 1988 by Tony Kushner

First published by B P P I in Janurary 1992 in PLAYS BY TONY KUSHNER

First acting edition: October 2003
I S B N: 0-88145-231-9

Book design: Marie Donovan
Word processing: Microsoft Word for Windows
Typographic controls: Xerox Ventura Publisher 2.0 P E
Typeface: Palatino
Printed and bound in the U S A

ORIGINAL PRODUCTION

THE ILLUSION was first presented by New York
Theater Workshop in October 1988. It was directed
by Brian Kulick, with the following cast:

PRIDAMANT .... Victor Radier-Wexler
THE AMANUENSIS .... Stephen Spinella
ALCANDRE .... Isaiah Whitlock, Jr
CALISTO/CLINDOR/THEOGENES ..... Michael Galardi
MELIBEA/ISABELLE/HIPPOLYTA .... Regina Taylor
ELICIA/LYSE/CLARINA .... Socorro Santiago
PLERIBO/ADRASTE/PRINCE FLORILAME ... Neil Maffin
MATAMORE .... Arthur Hanket

The play was subsequently performed, in the current
expanded version, at Hartford Stage Company in
January 1990, directed by Mark Lamos, with the
following cast: Marco St John, Jarlath Conroy, Frederick
Neumann, J Grant Albrecht, Ashley Gardner, Bellina
Logan, Andrew Coulteaux, and Phillip Goodwin.

It was next produced at the Los Angeles Theater Center
in April 1990, directed by David Schweitzer, with the
following cast: Alan Mandell, Tom Cayler, Mary
Woronov, Jonathan Silverman, Lea Thompson, Karole
Lynn Foreman, Mitchell Lichtenstein, and John Fleck.

CHARACTERS & SETTING

PRIDAMANT *of Avignon, a lawyer*
THE AMANUENSIS, *servant to* ALCANDRE *(also* GERONTE*)*
ALCANDRE, *a magician*
CALISTO/CLINDOR/THEOGENES, *son of* PRIDAMANT
MELIBEA/ISABELLE/HIPPOLYTA, *beloved/wife of* CALISTO/
   CLINDOR/THEOGENES
ELICIA/LYSE/CLARINA, *maid/friend of* MELIBEA/
   ISABELLE/HIPPOLYTA
PLERIBO/ADRASTE/PRINCE FLORILAME, *rival of*
   CALISTO/CLINDOR/THEOGENES
MATAMORE, *a lunatic*

The play takes place in the cave of the magician ALCANDRE
*during the 17th Century, near Remulac, a small town in the
south of France.*

AUTHOR'S NOTE

This version of *L'ILLUSION COMIQUE* was done for a production directed by Brian Kulick, who brought the play to my attention and asked me to adapt it. It owes much of its present structure and texture, as well as one of its best jokes, to him; Mark Lamos (the Emperor of Ice Cream) and Connie Congdon also provided great dramaturgical advice, inspiration, and concrete ideas; Nina Mankin was invaluable in getting it into playable shape; and it owes its second life to Greg Leaming's support. My deepest gratitude to them all.

THE ILLUSION
is for Brian Kulick,
collaborator and friend.

ACT ONE

(A man alone in a dark cave)

PRIDAMANT: Is this the cave of the magician Alcandre?
(Silence) Is this.... Nothing here. Hello? *(He strikes a match; it fizzles out.)* Hello!

(THE AMANUENSIS *appears, dressed in black, silent.)*

PRIDAMANT: Is this the cave of the magician Alcandre?
I'm a pilgrim in need of his services.

(Pause. No response from THE AMANUENSIS*)*

PRIDAMANT: Is your master in? Can you speak?
I followed the directions carefully, but I've arrived....
(Looks around, shrugs) I shouldn't have come at night,
I suppose, but to be honest I'm ashamed to be seen in
a place like this, wizards and spells, I...I'm Pridamant
of Avignon. *(Pause)* That name means nothing to you.
Well, it means something in Avignon. Assure your
master I can pay. More than adequately.

(Again a pause. THE AMANUENSIS *is silent and still.)*

PRIDAMANT: Say something! Move, fetch, announce me,
more light or... Very well, I must have the wrong
address. A thousand pardons and good night.

(PRIDAMANT *turns to leave.* THE AMANUENSIS *knocks
loudly on the floor.)*

VOICE: He doesn't speak because he has no tongue.

(PRIDAMANT *freezes. Another knock)*

VOICE: And because he's deaf he didn't catch your name.

PRIDAMANT: Pridamant. Of Avignon. I'm looking for the sorcerer Alcandre they told me lives in this dismal pit.

VOICE: Turn around.

(PRIDAMANT *does*. ALCANDRE *appears*.)

ALCANDRE: What do you want from him?

PRIDAMANT: Do I have the honor....

ALCANDRE: What do you want? This is close enough; my time is precious to me; your business, or go away.

PRIDAMANT: I want a more intimate consultation.

ALCANDRE: Furtive whispering.

PRIDAMANT: It's something personal.

ALCANDRE: So ashamed...

PRIDAMANT: I'm not ashamed of anything.

ALCANDRE: Then why not declare your business openly?

PRIDAMANT: (*Pausing, then, referring to* THE AMANUENSIS) Is he really deaf and dumb?

ALCANDRE: I did the surgery myself. I too have need of privacy. He is my servant; I keep his tongue in a jar. He serves me devotedly, all the better since I had his eardrums pierced. You are a troubled and unhappy man. What crimes have you committed? Confess.

(*Pause, then*)

PRIDAMANT: I destroyed my son. My only child. Years ago. When he was barely a step past being a boy. He seemed uncontrollable, wild, dangerous to me in all sorts of little ways. I loved him so much I wanted to

strangle him. I wanted to snap his spine sometimes in
a ferocious embrace. Everything about him seemed
calculated to drive me to distraction, and did.

ALCANDRE: You murdered your son?

PRIDAMANT: I might have; he ran before I had the
chance. Disappeared. Helped himself to as much
money and as many valuables as I'd left unlocked and
fled Avignon, and that was fifteen years ago. Since then
I've never had a word from or about him; hired agents
could unearth no trace; expensive information proved
worthless; I have paid through the nose for every clue
but always I am led to a blank, tall, doorless wall
through which he seems to have slipped. As if by magic.

ALCANDRE: Magic. Which explains your long journey
from Avignon to me.

PRIDAMANT: It's near-fatal for a man of my age and
poor physical condition; I never thought I'd make it.
I hear you can.... They tell me that you conjure. That
you can bring to bear on any situation certain skills and
lost arts of a pre-Christian variety....

ALCANDRE: Even if I could restore your son to you I
wouldn't. He's lucky to have escaped....

PRIDAMANT: But I've changed. For the first time this
year in the early spring I faced death in the form a
sharp, surprising tearing at my heart. A warning.
Nothing of my life for the past fifteen years is real to
me. I can't stop thinking about him. I can't face death
until I see him again. I want to tell him I love him.
I want to ask him why he never wrote. I want him to
know that the ghost of him has ruined my life, has
sucked dry everything, present happiness and memory
as well. I want to make him sick with guilt. I want to
make him the heir to my fortunes. He must be very
poor....

(Figures appear, dressed beautifully, frozen in a tableau.)

PRIDAMANT: Oh, impossible, impossible; it's him;
you've called him back to me.... My heart, as I told you,
I have to avoid excitement.

ALCANDRE: Odd for a man avoiding excitement to
come to a magician's cave at night. What did you
expect?

PRIDAMANT: Information. Memory restored. I don't
know. But safely, painlessly. Crystal balls and tea
leaves, not this...resurrection.

ALCANDRE: You're perfectly safe here.

(The tableau shifts. PRIDAMANT moves away quickly.)

ALCANDRE: Frightened?

PRIDAMANT: My son always frightens me. I want to
speak to him.

ALCANDRE: Uh-uh-uh. Violate the boundary between
their world and ours only at the greatest peril to
yourself. Cross over, and you may not be able to find
your way back.

PRIDAMANT: Then what am I to do?

ALCANDRE: Use your eyes, your ears, take from their
carryings-on whatever you can, these clouds of colored
vapor. Resign yourself, a fitful sleeper in the throes of a
nightmare, powerless to affect his life, a possibility you
relinquished years ago.... If he teeters on the brink of
some fatal trap, you can call out a warning; still he'll fall
in and die.

PRIDAMANT: I wouldn't want to see that.

ALCANDRE: I'll show you his life, just as he's lived it,
since you cast him off. How it ends, I cannot say.

PRIDAMANT: He's so young. He's hardly aged at all.

ALCANDRE: Before the night is through, he will. You see
him now as the young man you banished, years ago.
Life is still fresh to him. Full of wonders...

CALISTO: I have seen a most splendid vision.

PRIDAMANT: What's he talking about? Is he also a
magician?

ALCANDRE: He is frequently in love.

CALISTO: The vision's name is Melibea.

ALCANDRE: *(Pointing to* MELIBEA*)* That one there. Your
son's great passion, his waking dream. If we retreat, the
first phantasma can commence.

CALISTO: I was hungry;
I trapped a hawk, a little wire snare
Snatched it by the red foot and I said,
"That's dinner."
But it pleaded with me not to eat it, high heart and all,
So I released it after making a pact:
"I set you free; you find me other prey."
And I let go and in a panic it tore madly away;
I followed it; it led me here,
To your garden, Melibea,
More wonderful than freedom, or the air itself,
Where with the hungry eye of a hawk
I am watching your every move. My love.

PRIDAMANT: At home he always told stories like that.
When I could catch him, I'd whip him for telling lies.

CALISTO: This garden wall encircles paradise;
Within, Melibea waits; if I touch the stones,
I can feel her heart beating, and I know, I know
It's beating for me.
Melibea, Melibea,
Open the door of your garden wall.
It's cold out here; I'm freezing.

MELIBEA: It isn't cold, it's spring, and warm,
And I know who you are,
Calisto.

PRIDAMANT: Calisto? His name's not....

MELIBEA: You can't come in.

CALISTO: I'm in already.

MELIBEA: Only the sound of you—eventually
Your voice will give out.

CALISTO: My voice in your garden; my words in your
ears....

MELIBEA: My fingers in my ears; I'm deaf to your
prayers.

CALISTO: My words will linger till they spy a chance,
When your guard is lowered, to shower you with love.
Your voice is honey, even your contempt,
A sweet potent liquor I draw into my roots, then
I sprout green leaves atop my head
And blossom purple buds of desire for you.
Out here, Melibea, look out here,
Don't you want to see such a miraculous plant?
Come and shelter under me: I am a Melibeatree.

MELIBEA: You're silly and you're poor,
Calisto; I'm too busy for your games.
You make me nervous. Please go away.

CALISTO: I'll climb the wall.

MELIBEA: I'll call the gardener.

CALISTO: And let his blood water the roses....
Let me in or I'll stab my eyes out.

MELIBEA: Leave or I'll have you arrested. I don't
know you. You're excessive. And strange. Calisto.
That probably isn't even your real name.

PRIDAMANT: It isn't! His name isn't Calisto, it's....

AMANUENSIS: *(Fiercely and rather frighteningly)*
Sssssshhhhh!

ALCANDRE: Sssshhh. Sit and don't move. Watch and
don't talk.

MELIBEA: Calisto. Like from some old romance.

PRIDAMANT: But I must interrupt, please. Something's
wrong, something's off; it looks like him, but they've
got the name wrong.

ALCANDRE: What do you mean, wrong? Wrong
according to whom? It isn't wrong, it's what it is,
it's what it has to be; Calisto, it's the perfect name for
him, shapely, strong, open-ended, with a little bite, I...
There are always these small discrepancies between
vision and memory. Concentrate on the general outline,
leave the details to me. And keep quiet.

PRIDAMANT: She thinks he's an impostor. Perhaps the
new name is as false as the fancy getup.

ALCANDRE: Yes, yes, perhaps, watch and see.

MELIBEA: You're an impostor. I'm sorry you're so
miserable, but it's not my fault.

CALISTO: It is, it is.

MELIBEA: I'm done with you.

CALISTO: I'll die out here.

MELIBEA: Die and decay, you garden pest. Elicia!

(ELICIA enters.)

ELICIA: Ma'am?

MELIBEA: Make sure that leper stays outside. If he tries
to breech the barricades, shoot him dead.

ELICIA: Between the eyes.

(As MELIBEA exits.)

ELICIA: My aim is true. You can always depend on your trusty maid.

(MELIBEA *is gone.* ELICIA *opens the garden door.*)

ELICIA: Let's have a look.
Uh, God, another one!

CALISTO: Another what?

ELICIA: Another suitor. Each day there are more.
They're dropping from the trees like the apples of autumn, just as wormy, most of them are, just as overripe....

CALISTO: If I have rivals, I have to fight them.

ELICIA: There's just one other roundabout today,
Well bred, polite, a charming man.

CALISTO: I was trying to be charming. It didn't work.
She hates me now.

ELICIA: Well...

CALISTO: She does, she does, she hates me now; I'll die,
I will, I can't live without her.

ELICIA: You saw her yesterday for the very first time.
You've spoken to her twice.
You lived before you met her, and
You'll live for years to come.

CALISTO: I won't.

ELICIA: You will. You look perfectly healthy.

CALISTO: I only look that way; inside, I bleed.

ELICIA: And so does she.

CALISTO: She...suffers?

ELICIA: Dreadfully.

CALISTO: Because...?

ELICIA: A man.

CALISTO: ...Who causes her pain?

ELICIA: Night and day.

CALISTO: Show me; I'll kill him; I'll tear out his heart
And offer it up as a present to her,
A savage token of my barbaric love!

ELICIA: Savage, barbaric, but not very bright!
It's you, you fool, you lunatic, you lout.
You're her persecutor, she aches for you.

CALISTO: No.

ELICIA: Yes.

CALISTO: No.

ELICIA: Yes.

CALISTO: Yes?

ELICIA: Yes.

CALISTO: Yes! How do you know?

ELICIA: Oh, we maids know these things about our
mistresses;
We're in and out of their lives like bees in lilies,
Tidying up more than their bedclothes and their hair.
She didn't have you arrested.

CALISTO: She threatened to.

ELICIA: But she didn't. I would have. She didn't.
You're alarming. Wild. How can she resist you?
You have such pretty teeth. Each one
Like a little kernel of white corn.
Here she comes: hide in the bush;
She's on the brink: I'll give a push.
(Aside) She's ready to fall for him head over heels;
And why am I helping? I know how he feels.
When passion possesses, you freeze and you burn,
Your bedsheets get knotted; you toss and you turn;
Your laundry gets soiled, you tear out your hair,

So I'm helping out; and why should I care?
I find him attractive; and intrigue is fun,
And a surrogate love affair's better than none.

(MELIBEA *enters.*)

MELIBEA: Who are you talking to, Elicia?
I thought I warned you to keep the door shut.

ELICIA: There's a gentleman, ma'am.
He's lying out here. On the ground,
Writhing and flailing in some kind of mortal agony,
Making terrible, terrible sounds.

MELIBEA: Oh, let me see. (*She looks.*)
There's no one here.

ELICIA: He's disappeared.

MELIBEA: Maybe he got better and went away.
Or maybe he crawled into a bush to die. We could
start beating the bushes, I suppose.

ELICIA: Spare the poor bushes. Wherever he's crawled,
we'll hear him moaning. He moaned very strangely,
the poor, poor man.

MELIBEA: Strangely?

ELICIA: Yes. Each moan sounded like someone's name.
Yours, in fact. Just like this:
"MMMMMMMelib-b-b-eeeeaaaahh!",
"MMMMMMelib-b-b-eeeeeeeeaaaahhh!"

MELIBEA: Oh! Oh! Calisto! It was Calisto! He's found
yet another way to make a spectacle of himself! Another
way to drag my name through the mud! Calisto! That
troll! That fountain of dreadful metaphors! (*She kneels.*)
Please, Holy Father, please, Blessed Mother of God,
what crime did I commit that you should send this
demon to torture me? Make him go away! He frightens
me! I hate him! I hate him! I hate him, I hate him, I hate
him!

CALISTO: *(To* ELICIA, *from the bush)* It's going very well. Congratulations.

ELICIA: *(To* CALISTO*)* Back in the bush. I'm not done yet. *(To* MELIBEA*)* I know just what you mean, ma'am. The minute I saw him I said to myself, "I hate that man". For one thing, he's so ugly.

MELIBEA: Isn't he?

ELICIA: Remarkably ugly. Warty like a squash. Greasy. Fat. The ugliest man I ever saw.

MELIBEA: Well, not so ugly as that, but....

ELICIA: Ugly enough. And incredibly stupid!

MELIBEA: Stupid?

ELICIA: A veritable clod of earth; an ox could outsmart him.

MELIBEA: I thought he spoke well.

ELICIA: Sure, if you like hearing gibberish.

MELIBEA: It wasn't all gibberish.

ELICIA: Oh, please, ma'am, your natural generosity carries you away.

MELIBEA: I am not naturally generous; it's just that he....

ELICIA: All that hot air! *(Imitating* CALISTO*)* "Melibea! So fair! Radiant! Divine! Beautiful Melibea! Little star of the dawn!"

MELIBEA: Actually I liked the part about the little star of the dawn.

ELICIA: You're far too sensible to fall for that stuff. I mean obviously you aren't worthy of such intense, passionate adoration.

MELIBEA: What do you mean by that?

ELICIA: Well, it's obvious.

MELIBEA: Oh, really?

ELICIA: I mean, you're perfectly nice and all, but you're not exactly the little star of the dawn.

MELIBEA: Well, he thought I am.

ELICIA: But he's a troll.

MELIBEA: No! I mean, yes, but...

ELICIA: But?

MELIBEA: But...

ELICIA: But there are worse things than trolls.

MELIBEA: Many worse things.

ELICIA: Trolls are...well, unusual!

MELIBEA: They are! And sweet.

ELICIA: Sweet, yes, maybe a little.

MELIBEA: Who? Calisto?

ELICIA: Maybe a little?

MELIBEA: Maybe...

ELICIA: A little?

MELIBEA: A little. Yes.

ELICIA: And he'd probably be better behaved and sweeter still if it weren't for that toothache.

MELIBEA: Toothache? He has a toothache?

ELICIA: Oh, yes, didn't you know, a horrible toothache, for eight days running.

MELIBEA: Oh, how dreadful. There's nothing worse than a toothache.

ELICIA: Nothing. His manservant tells me....

MELIBEA: Yes?

ELICIA: That to ease his terrible pain...

MELIBEA: The toothache...

ELICIA: The toothache.

MELIBEA: Yes?

ELICIA: He sings.

MELIBEA: Oh...

ELICIA: And plays the lute...

MELIBEA: I love the lute.

ELICIA: And that the countryside for miles around
Grows peaceful with the bright response of birds,
And, playing and singing, handsome as a god,
He isn't even Calisto anymore.
He is like Orpheus.

MELIBEA: He is Orpheus! And I am his Euridyce!
Rescue me from hell!

ELICIA: Pardon?

MELIBEA: I said I don't feel well. I'm going to my room.

ELICIA: If I see him again, maybe I could give him your handkerchief.

MELIBEA: My handkerchief?

ELICIA: He could use it to wipe his fevered brow. Or I could wipe it for him.

MELIBEA: DON'T YOU DARE! I mean, let him wipe his own brow. I mean, here.... *(Giving her the handkerchief)* I have to go to my room, I can't breathe.... *(She exits.)*

CALISTO: *(Entering from the bush)* It's strange.

ELICIA: Very strange...I did better than I expected.
I nearly convinced myself.

CALISTO: It's destiny.
(Taking the handkerchief)
I'm the child of fortune, Elicia;

The orphan child of fate.
I was cast out; the wind blew me here
On great brown wings; and I always knew
She'd rescue me; she had no choice
But to love me.

ELICIA: I almost feel sorry for her. You look hungry.

CALISTO: Starving. But I think I'm about to be fed.

ELICIA: Ha-ha.

CALISTO: Ha-ha. Your eyes are pretty when you laugh.

ELICIA: You will be true to her, won't you?
I have a heart....

CALISTO: Attractively enshrined...

ELICIA: And I feel responsible, since I've set her up.

CALISTO: My every thought is of Melibea.
My eyes, my eyes are all for her.

ELICIA: Sweet Calisto, your eyes are very dark.

CALISTO: Like my father's—deep, dark, there's nothing
but love in them.

PRIDAMANT: That's the look! See? In his eyes! The look
that said danger to me. A thousand times since the day
he ran away I asked myself, "Did I imagine that look?"
but there it is. It makes my blood run cold. I am glad to
have seen this. His feral stare, like a wounded animal,
dangerous, with teeth.... What might he have done to
me if I hadn't driven him out?

ALCANDRE: He's merely in love with his Melibea.
That's a look of love.

PRIDAMANT: Love, yes, but what does love mean?
Nothing. Anything can be called love, any sort of
emotion. I find myself enjoying this vision, this
vindication. It's delectable. Memory without pain. Like

eating a great deal of delicious food without the
concomitant indigestion.

ALCANDRE: As if you'd lived a life you never really
lived.

PRIDAMANT: It makes me feel immortal. Please,
continue. I watch gluttonously.

ELICIA: I will bring her to you,
Who is yours by fate.
I think she's simmered long enough,
And should be ripe for eating. Poor little bird. *(Exits)*

CALISTO: The sun is setting!
Just for me!
The moon is rising! Just for me!
My happy heart's crawled up inside my mouth;
It lies there like a frog,
Amphibiously glad to see the night descend,
Bubbling the name of my beloved:
"MMMMMelibbbea. MMMMMelibbbea. MMMMM..."
Heaven sparkles, mad with joy,
The earth spins round an ache.
I am its core, its point, its pearl—
I want, therefore it spins.

*(CALISTO starts to hide. PLERIBO enters. CALISTO stops.
They stare at each other, at first with a kind of confused
recognition, and then with growing animosity.)*

CALISTO: Who are you?

PRIDAMANT: Ah, it must be my son's rival, looking for
his lover; poor fool; against this sharp-billed shrike he
doesn't stand a chance.

PLERIBO: Who are you?

CALISTO: Calisto. Who loves Melibea more
Than he loves himself, or God,
Or the world, or all the world's riches.

PLERIBO: Pleribo. Who loves Melibea more than that.

CALISTO: I love her so much that if she asked me to cut off my hand I'd do it.

PLERIBO: Well, I love her so much that if she asked me to cut off one hand I'd cut them both off.

CALISTO: Well, I love her so much that if she asked me to cut off both hands but she didn't really want me to I'd do it anyway.

PLERIBO: Well, I'd do it too and I'd also cut off my feet.

CALISTO: Would you really do that?

PLERIBO: No. I mean, not really. I mean, who would do something like that?

CALISTO: *(Meaning it)* I would.

(Little pause)

PLERIBO: This is a private garden. You'd better leave.

CALISTO: Make me.

PLERIBO: Uh, I forgot something inside. *(He starts to exit.)*

CALISTO: *(Stepping in front of him)* No.

(CALISTO *slaps* PLERIBO.)

CALISTO: If you love Melibea, fight for her.

PLERIBO: *(Near tears)* But I don't want to fight you.

CALISTO: You have to. We're rivals.

PLERIBO: That really hurt! That really hurt! You...hurt me!

(PLERIBO *stares at* CALISTO, *then lunges at him.* CALISTO *knocks him easily to the ground.)*

CALISTO: *(Crouching beside the prostrate* PLERIBO) I did?

PLERIBO: Yes. I've never been hit before.

CALISTO: I could keep hitting you. And it would hurt
more and more. But do you know what will make the
pain completely unbearable?

(PLERIBO *shakes his head "No".)*

CALISTO: Melibea will come through that door soon.
She'll see you beaten. It hurts to be hit. It will hurt much
much more to be thoroughly humiliated in front of her.
Don't you agree?

(PLERIBO *doesn't answer.)*

CALISTO: So I'm going to turn my back, and you can
leave. Better hurry, because I hear her coming down.
If I turn around and you're still there, it will be very
unpleasant for you. Take my word for it.

(CALISTO *turns his back.* PLERIBO *hesitates, then crawls
away.)*

CALISTO: My first rival bested!
It wasn't so hard; and well-timed,
My Melibea of the moon is coming.
I'll hide and await my cue. *(He hides.)*

(MELIBEA *and* ELICIA *enter.)*

MELIBEA: Is it safe? No one here?

ELICIA: No, ma'am, no sign of Ca...

MELIBEA: Ssshhhh!!! Please, for the love of God,
Speak that name only to murder me.

ELICIA: What's wrong with you, ma'am?

MELIBEA: I have a fever. I thought the night air
Would cool it down; it makes it worse.
I hurt.

ELICIA: Where's the pain?

MELIBEA: It starts here. *(Indicates her heart)* And then it
spreads throughout. I have aches and chills in places
I've never felt achy or chilly before. Am I dying?

ELICIA: Probably not. Where God gives a wound
He also gives a remedy;
As it hurts, so it heals. I know
The very medicine for this malady.

MELIBEA: Is it a plant? Does it grow in the garden?
Is it nearby?

ELICIA: Very near.

MELIBEA: Pluck it, please, and bring it to me...

(ELICIA hands MELIBEA to CALISTO.)

MELIBEA: Oh!

CALISTO: Melibea.

MELIBEA: Calisto.

CALISTO: You aren't drawing away.

MELIBEA: I can't.

(The hawk's cry is heard.)

CALISTO: Look! See that shadow flying?

MELIBEA: Oh, a hawk!
What a sound it makes.
Every animal in the whole moonlit world
Freezes when it hears that cry.
It's like an icicle through the heart.

CALISTO: Are you shivering?

MELIBEA: It's cold.

CALISTO: Melibea. The source of fire is here in me;
Put your hand on my heart.

MELIBEA: *(Does this and then pulls her hand away)*
It's like a burning coal.
How strange, Calisto.

CALISTO: You are the answer to my every need.
I'll keep you warm, you'll save me from burning;
Both winter ice and blistering sun
Will be ours to command.
The winds will blow wild over our happiness....

(They kiss. ELICIA *runs in, breathless.)*

ELICIA: You'll have to run! Pleribo's told your father!
He's arming the gardeners with shovels and spades!

MELIBEA: Calisto!

CALISTO: In my imagination and in my speeches
I have slain a hundred gardeners!
What are these real gardeners
To the monstrous horticulturists
I have vanquished?

ELICIA: For Melibea's sake, you have to flee from here!
Leave her, please, her father is dangerous, and
The law is clear and very harsh!
For her sake, if not for yours!

CALISTO: I will return! Wait for me, my own adored!
With my great love for you...

(The theater goes completely black.)

PRIDAMANT: What happened? Magician? Hello?
The visions have disappeared! Just as the father
was about to enter! A light, please, I'm blind....

(There is a tick-tock noise. A dim light comes up.
PRIDAMANT *is alone with* THE AMANUENSIS, *who is
making the tick-tock noise with his tongue.* ALCANDRE
appears.)

ALCANDRE: Don't be alarmed. A great leap is taking
place. Days, months, years perhaps...

PRIDAMANT: But the father was about to appear.

ALCANDRE: Irrelevant to the story.

PRIDAMANT: Your servant. That noise. He...

ALCANDRE: Yes?

PRIDAMANT: He... Why is he doing that?

ALCANDRE: To indicate the passage of time.

PRIDAMANT: But... He's making the sound with his tongue.

ALCANDRE: Yes.

PRIDAMANT: You said he doesn't have a tongue.

ALCANDRE: Now he does.

PRIDAMANT: That's impossible.

ALCANDRE: If I can bring back your son I can restore a simple little tongue. Check your pocketwatch against him; you'll find he's remarkably accurate.

PRIDAMANT: Can he hear as well?

ALCANDRE: Naturally, he'll need a functional pair of ears to effectively participate in the vision about to unfold.

PRIDAMANT: Participate? But we can't enter their world! You said....

ALCANDRE: I said it was dangerous. And it is. But it can be done. I used to do it all the time. Finally I grew too old, acquired this hobgoblin; now, when it's necessary to cross over, I fling him into the chasm instead of going in myself. Would you care to try it? Join your son in his shadowy habitation?

PRIDAMANT: Absolutely not. I'm staying here.

ALCANDRE: No, no, of course not, consumption,
spectation, scrutiny, not participation, a wise choice,
mi padrone. We begin again.

(The tableau for Part Two appears: MATAMORE *and*
CLINDOR.*)*

PRIDAMANT: My son looks different. Has he aged?
His clothes are richer. No, I was wrong, it's not my son.
Calisto's coming now....

CLINDOR: *(To* MATAMORE*)* Your servant, Clindor.

PRIDAMANT: Clindor? This is my son, Calisto.

ALCANDRE: You said his name wasn't Calisto. I wish
you'd make up your mind.

CLINDOR: Master, it amazes me,
Titan, whose countenance
Is the world's great terror,
You've scaled the loftiest
Pinnacles of glory, and still you
Dream of conquest. Do you never rest?

MATAMORE: Never, slave, and now I must decide
Whose kingdom I should next acquire,
The King of Crete's or the Queen of Britain's?

CLINDOR: Both are island kingdoms; you would need
A navy of a thousand ships and
Ten thousand men to sail them.

MATAMORE: Ships? Men? I need no ships.
I'll swim the Hellespont on Monday
And the Channel Tuesday morning. And as for troops
I need none, other than
This mighty arm...

CLINDOR: Mighty indeed!

MATAMORE: ...And this fist of tempered steel.
I crushed the hearts of the Pashas of Ranjapoor
And battered down the cypress gates of Sinabar

With little else. The splinters like spears
Slew the gate's defenders by the dozens,
And with the hinges I cracked chariot and shield of
A hundred hundred knights. The blood ran
Ankle deep; it's not a thing
I like to talk about. Let Crete and Britain
Look to heaven: Matamore is near!

CLINDOR: Oh, let them live, great Master, you
Have more than gold and land enough.

MATAMORE: Half the planet.

CLINDOR: More than half. I spoke before
Of conquests sweeter but
More difficult to win....

MATAMORE: You speak of Isabelle. My genius
Leaps pages ahead to grasp your meaning.

CLINDOR: I bow before your protean brow.

MATAMORE: Then speak of Isabelle, but do not speak
Of difficult conquest. I know: My visage frights
The moguls and viziers: A fearsome face,
An awful, horrible, ghastly face,
A face that has sunk a thousand ships,
And made six hundred oxen run bellowing into the sea!
But look: I can transform this mask of Mars
To something of transplendent, masculine
Yet gentle beauty. *(He does this.)*

CLINDOR: Sorcery. You are as invincible, I see,
In battles of the heart as of the sword,
And not even the proudest woman could resist you;
Aphrodite herself would collapse at your feet.

MATAMORE: She did, in fact, and begged for me.

CLINDOR: But you spurned her.

MATAMORE: Utterly.
She interfered with my military campaigns.

Always clinging, eager for amour.
Since then I'm more careful displaying
My face of love.

CLINDOR: Temperate and wise!
But don your face, my godlike lord,
For Isabelle is near!

MATAMORE: Isabelle! You gave to her
The sonnets I indicted to her beauty?

CLINDOR: I did, my liege.

MATAMORE: And what was her response?

CLINDOR: She read them carefully, and wept.

MATAMORE: Tears of joy, no doubt. And here she
comes, I... She is accompanied by my rival; Like a tick,
he clings to her inseparably. *(Starts to exit)*

CLINDOR: Where are you going, scourge of heaven?

MATAMORE: He's a weak man, and weak men are
foolish.
He might be tempted to challenge me.

CLINDOR: Then you could obliterate him.

MATAMORE: I never fight with my love face on,
I worry that it might get scratched.

CLINDOR: Put on your terrible mask of war, then,
and slaughter him.

MATAMORE: What? With Isabelle so near?
Are you mad?
My mask of Mars clapped on my face
I'm fiercer than the tusked boar
And I might gore them both,
Skewering my love and rival both.

CLINDOR: I spoke rashly. Perhaps we should retire
instead.

MATAMORE: Perhaps we should. I'll lead the way.

(They exit. ISABELLE *and* ADRASTE *enter.)*

ADRASTE: I have devoted myself entirely
To discovering the sight, the sound,
The word that will finally awaken you
To my devotion, the word that will set marvels free.
But nothing penetrates your shrouded heart.

ISABELLE: Those who don't understand the world
Think words have meanings that adhere
With constancy; you offer me a thing
And say it is a rose; to you, no doubt,
It is. To me it's a thistle,
And I'm pricked by its thorns.
You say you love me; I say you torment me.
You describe me at great length, and
I know you think I'm flattered;
In point of fact I'm bored.

ADRASTE: When a kind word from you
Would be life's blood to me,
You're silent as the dead.
You only speak to heap scorn on my love.

ISABELLE: I only speak to tell you how I feel.
I have no more feeling for you, Adraste,
Than the dead have for anything;
I'm insensate; for God's sake
Let me rest in peace.

ADRASTE: You ought to pity me, at least.

ISABELLE: I do.

ADRASTE: And should I live on that? Pity,
When I'm ravenous for your love?

ISABELLE: You may be ravenous; I have no food to give.
I do pity you. Your pain's unnecessary and absurd.
I don't mean to bruise your tenderness

With my harshness, but please know, Adraste,
That I cannot love you, do not love you,
And want nothing other than your absence.
Only your persistence makes us enemies.

ADRASTE: Enemies. You will never be an enemy of mine,
Isabelle. I loved you long before we ever met;
We two are torn halves of one whole that existed
In some earlier, better world than this.
You defy all of heaven's designs if you refuse to love
me.

ISABELLE: Then I defy them; tell heaven to stop asking
me
To do impossible things.

ADRASTE: Listen to me, Isabelle.
Your father's chosen me, you know he has;
I have to have you; if not through love,
I'll invoke the law and his paternal right
To settle your affairs as he sees fit.

ISABELLE: That's a dead end and a desperate move.
If I'm taken as goods, traded
With a handshake and a bill of sale, I promise you
That I will poison both
Your bed and your life with my hatred of you.

ADRASTE: A quick death with you in a poisoned bed
Is better than living alone.
I'll take my chances.
Your father's walking in his garden.
I'll close the deal.
The bill of sale was drawn up long ago.

ISABELLE: Please, Adraste...

ADRASTE: You pity me.
I can't be guided by pity for you.
My love's too fierce; it won't permit me to

Pity the woman who hates my love.
I go now to claim you: my murderer; my bride.
PRIDAMANT: I'm utterly bewildered. It's uncanny.
Why has everyone changed their name?
ALCANDRE: You still pick after tiny details, like a lawyer
examining a brief.
PRIDAMANT: I am a lawyer. A man has a right to expect
coherence....
ALCANDRE: Expect nothing from these visions you can't
expect from life.
I gave up hoping for coherence years ago....

(MATAMORE *and* CLINDOR *reenter.*)

MATAMORE: Madam, do not be alarmed
To see your gutless suitor fled away.
He saw me coming....
ISABELLE: And instantly ran.
He shows better sense in this
Than I'd have guessed him capable.

CLINDOR: Kings and emperors, after all,
Would do no less.

ISABELLE: When Matamore approaches,
Everyone retreats; in fact,
I feel an urge myself....

MATAMORE: It's natural to flee me; I am so great,
At times I want to flee myself;
But stay with me; I'll extemporize
Another sonnet to your grace.

ISABELLE: Oh, don't do that! I mean, not while
The sweet music of the other twelve you wrote
Is still ringing in my ears; let me savor that.

MATAMORE: You're as beautiful as you are wise!
An excess of sweetness is as disagreeable

As a lack of bitter gall. Hmmmm.
That's rather good! Delamont!

CLINDOR: Um, it's Clindor, sir.

MATAMORE: Delamont, record that last remark.
(To ISABELLE*)* I'm collecting
My pithiest sayings in a book.

CLINDOR: *(Writing)* This one, sir, is full of pith.

MATAMORE: Thank you. Read it back to me.

CLINDOR: "An excess of sweetness is as disagreeable
As a lack of bitter gall."

MATAMORE: My God, that's good. One problem,
though.

ISABELLE: What's that?

MATAMORE: It makes no sense.
Ah, well, I'll have to work on it.

ISABELLE: Oh, do! Polish it up, in some private place,
And give it to me as a present.
I adore a well-polished epigram.

MATAMORE: I have a thousand others....

ISABELLE: No. I want this one. Go. To work.
Your messenger of love
Can stay with me and press your advantage
While you wrestle with your muse.

MATAMORE: I will buff it to a brilliance, and make it
shine
So that you can see yourself reflected in its biting wit.
Delamont...

CLINDOR: Clindor.

MATAMORE: Whatever. If the Queen of Iceland should
arrive,
Tell her I am indisposed.

ISABELLE: The Queen of Iceland?

MATAMORE: Will not let me rest; pursues me in her sled;
And wants my fiery love to thaw
Her frozen marriage bed.
Also good. Write it down, Delamont,
I'm off to shine my epigram. *(Exits)*

CLINDOR: It will take several years, I think,
To make that saying shine.

ISABELLE: Then we shall have to amuse ourselves while
he's away.
Can you, messenger of love, amuse me for as long as
that?

CLINDOR: For several years? Without a doubt.

ISABELLE: Begin, then, I need to be amused.

CLINDOR: I'll tell you a story.

ISABELLE: Is the story fact or fantasy?

CLINDOR: Does it matter?

ISABELLE: Yes, I've heard too many fantasies today.
Tell me something true.

CLINDOR: Once there was a servant,
Without land or means or title, poor, an orphan,
Forced from his home by an unloving father,
Who found employment with a lunatic squire
To act as his bootblack, his secretary
And more. To deliver messages of love.
To a beautiful lady.

ISABELLE: This is a sad story; I'm intrigued but not
amused.

CLINDOR: It gets sadder still. Can you guess
What soon befell this poor young Mercury?

ISABELLE: Tell me.

CLINDOR: He went one day to deliver a letter to the lady
And unexpectedly delivered his heart instead.

ISABELLE: Did the lady accept it?

CLINDOR: I've forgotten how it ends.
Do you think she did?

ISABELLE: Yes. I do.

CLINDOR: Even though the messenger
Had never told her of his love before?

ISABELLE: Oh, but he had. With a tongue of air, a quiet
voice,
That spoke truer, clearer, finer words
Than any she'd heard in all the endless vocalizing
Of a dozen braying lords. It did not brag, lie,
Flatter, or threaten, this quiet voice,
But it sang a silent hymn of adoration
Only her heart could hear.

CLINDOR: And then what happened?

ISABELLE: I suppose
They fell deeply, completely in love.

CLINDOR: The story's improving. Maybe it ends happily.

ISABELLE: Maybe. There's a rival.

CLINDOR: There always is a rival.

ISABELLE: And a father who forbids their love.

CLINDOR: Fathers, too, have a habit of becoming
The very nemeses of love.

ISABELLE: What hope for a good conclusion, then,
With obstacles like these?

CLINDOR: Obstacles are only obstacles
Until they're overcome.
In all such stories,
The lovers exchange

Some token of their passion;
Traditionally, it seems to me, a kiss....

ISABELLE: I never defy tradition
Unless I'm driven to....

(They kiss.)

ISABELLE: My father's choice is made;
Now I make mine. I love you.
My father's very strong;
I'm stronger. And I will have my way.

(ADRASTE *enters.)*

ISABELLE: *(To* CLINDOR*)* Tell your master I refuse his
advances;
My heart is occupied with other matters;
I'll send my maid down with a letter,
Explaining the vagaries, the strange fortunes of love.
(Exits)

ADRASTE: I can't help but envy your fortune,
Boy. Isabelle, who flees when I approach,
As though a sudden rainstorm had spoiled the day,
Was listening very carefully to you.
One wonders what you have to say to her.

CLINDOR: Only what my master Matamore
Would like me to convey.

ADRASTE: I think it would be better if your master
Took his madness and its messenger
Somewhere else.

CLINDOR: My master, sir, is harmless;
He can't compete with you.

ADRASTE: You seem intelligent, a decent sort of man.
It's inexplicable that you should serve
This monster of ego run amok; no poverty
Or need for gold could justify this servitude.

CLINDOR: You're rich, sir, and have never felt
The need for gold;
I respectfully suggest you have no idea
What sorts of things poverty justifies.

ADRASTE: I don't trust you; and I respectfully request
I never see you here again;

CLINDOR: It's hardly fitting, my lord,
For you to feel so threatened by a man of my low rank.

ADRASTE: I don't feel threatened;
I've already won the prize.
Her father's signed a wedding pact with me.
Your master's a pest, but he makes me laugh.
You I don't find funny in the least.
Climbers and pretenders never are.

CLINDOR: Someday you'll be sorry you said that.

ADRASTE: Are you threatening me?

CLINDOR: No. I'm prophesying, sir, a gift I have.
I take my leave, with your permission.

ADRASTE: Granted instantly.
And may swift winds blow you on your voyage hence.

(CLINDOR *exits.* LYSE *enters.*)

LYSE: You spoke with him?

ADRASTE: I did.

LYSE: And now you see you were mistaken.

ADRASTE: On the contrary. I'm all the more convinced.
She's fond of this servant.

LYSE: She is.

ADRASTE: That's more than you'd confess before.

LYSE: I'm sorry for you, sir. I am. And, I admit, I had
some hand in shaping her opinion of this man.

ADRASTE: What is her opinion?
I want the truth.
Is it as bad as I think it is?

LYSE: *(Showing the letter)* You'll spare the bearer of bad
news?

ADRASTE: What's in the letter you hold in your hand?

LYSE: She worships him. He's all her heart.
As much as Matamore amuses her,
As coldly as she feels towards you,
So much and more does she entirely yearn for him.
She's sick with love.

ADRASTE: Then let her sicken and die!
I'll kill her for this treason!
I...
It's disgraceful for a lady of her rank
To throw herself on paupers.

LYSE: He tells me that his father's rich,
But they're estranged; he says all sorts of things.
He pretends to be a simple sort of servant, but
He can talk like the devil, beautiful words,
And he scatters them freely, in every direction.
He can make you forget
Where you stop and he begins,
And after five minutes' conversation you find
That you're breathing in tempo with him. It's eerie.
I'm worried. For my mistress's sake.

ADRASTE: Your loyalty's impressive, Lyse. Is it for sale?

LYSE: Not on the open market, but for a good cause...

ADRASTE *(Giving her a diamond)* Will this do as a deposit?

LYSE: Handsomely. I'm all for you.

ADRASTE: I want to catch them making love.

LYSE: Easily arranged. They rendezvous down at the
arbor in fifteen minutes. You'll find them together.
Will Clindor be hurt?

ADRASTE: Yes. I promise you that.
If I can return my pain to its wellspring,
I'll do it happily. And if he feels
Even a drop of what I've suffered,
He'll carry the scars till his dying day. *(Exits)*

LYSE: By this betrayal I bait the trap;
When its jaws snap shut, Clindor will bleed.
It's not for the love of a glittering stone
That I set the stage for this bloody deed....
I only seek justice, to punish a sinner—
And now comes the cat—sniffing for dinner.
I'll be a cold Fury in my fatal resolve.

(CLINDOR enters.)

LYSE: Good morning, sir, did you sleep well last night?

CLINDOR: Like a statue, Lyse.
I didn't stir once; the sheets on the bed
Weren't even wrinkled....

LYSE: Now isn't that odd?
When I left your room, all of the linen
Was thoroughly mussed.

CLINDOR: But after you'd gone,
I smoothed everything over;
Like magic the bed looked
Like it hadn't been touched;
And with your smell trapped
On my hands and my sheets,
I drifted off to the sweetest slumber.

LYSE: I'm glad I helped you to a good night's sleep.

CLINDOR: You have a letter. Is it for me?

LYSE: No. It's addressed
"To My One Faithful Love."
And since it's from Isabelle,
It can't be for you.

CLINDOR: Are you angry?

LYSE: Oh, no. Not angry, darling Clindor;
I've discovered a new feeling,
One that has no name. My heart is full of it;
If I could make a broth,
With my heart as the meat stock
And this feeling as the spice,
One sip would curl your lips back from your pretty face
And send you straight to hell.
But I'm not angry.

CLINDOR: I haven't been untrue to you.

LYSE: Isabelle would be surprised to hear you say that.
I'm a little taken aback myself.

CLINDOR: I love you both equally.

LYSE: Oh, what nonsense.

CLINDOR: I do, Lyse, I do. Equally, but differently.

LYSE: Equally but differently. Her sparkling eyes,
my dainty foot...

CLINDOR: Your beauty and her money.

LYSE: I see. Well, that's blunt.

CLINDOR: I won't insult you by telling you stories.
I could easily spend a century or two in bed with you.
But...

LYSE: But you can't live on that. Do as you intend to do:
Go where
the money is.

CLINDOR: My desire's all for you.
But all you have to offer is desire.

I do desire Isabelle, and also
All that Isabelle affords:
I'm tired of being poor.
You have nothing, I have less than that.
Two zeroes equal zero.
It's simple mathematics.

LYSE: The worst thing is,
Your schemes make sense to me.
Marry money; I'd do the same....

CLINDOR: Love in poverty's short-lived;
Poor and married we'd soon fall out of love.
You understand.

LYSE: God help me, I do.

CLINDOR: I knew you would. The letter, please.

(She gives it to him.)

CLINDOR: She'll meet me?

LYSE: In the arbor.

CLINDOR: I'll go there and wait for her.
You're so beautiful it's dangerous to stay.
My love might get the best of me
And spoil everything. *(Exits)*

LYSE: The best of you. Now there's a laugh.
I've had your best, and you've had mine
And used me up and cast me off; your best,
You bastard, looks to me
No better than your worst.
He thinks he's now a little god
In the golden shrine of Isabelle's heart;
I'll tip him out, this serving man,
And watch him tumble down;
As he pricks, this trickster, let him pay!
As he plays his changes on the theme of love
Oh, change his pleasure into pain, and let him lose

The thread of his unholy variations! Justice
And unhappiness!
That's how it has to end.

PRIDAMANT: They're all in league against him! I don't
want to watch anymore.

ALCANDRE: But he's your son. Surely you want to see
how he fares in this sea of sharks.

PRIDAMANT: Not really, no. It's too upsetting, and I
don't like what's going on.

ALCANDRE: But it's history, it's memory, it's all already
happened, and your closing your eyes can't alter that—

PRIDAMANT: I can leave!

ALCANDRE: Oh, well, your tricky heart, I understand;
the tension, you find this bit too alarming, it agitates
unnecessarily—allow me to make a small adjustment....

(He motions in the air, and LYSE *is struck by a sudden
change of heart.)*

LYSE: On the other hand:
If revenge tastes sweet, as they say it does,
Does this taste so like brass because
As much as I'd love to spoil his plan
I'm still in love with this catlike man
Whose cruelty's all of an animal kind,
A matter of muscle, rather than mind,
And though he deserves to be knocked down flat,
There's nothing accomplished by killing the cat.
I must recant my treason,
Unravel the weave of this deadly design,
Undo what I've done....

*(*MATAMORE *enters.)*

MATAMORE: I have it, I have it, my epigram,
Sweet Isabelle, I....

LYSE: And for that purpose,
Here comes the very King of Undoing.

MATAMORE: Ha. Isabelle gone. Her scullion, alone.
What's become of your mistress, scullion?

LYSE: My mistress, Sir, has become....
I cannot say it.

MATAMORE: Your reticence is commendable, jade.
But speak. You must;
For Matamore's gaping ears
Even the stumps of trees divulge
Such secrets as tree stumps possess.
Tell me, poppet, where's she gone.
That gleaming, beaming, peerless wonder?

LYSE: She's down in the arbor making love to your
servant.

MATAMORE: I beg your pardon?

LYSE: Isabelle, that gleaming, beaming wonder,
Is at this moment in the arbor with your serving man,
And they're not pressing grapes.

MATAMORE: Do you mean to imply...?

LYSE: I do.

MATAMORE: Affronterous pimple!
Presumptuous homuncula!
Foul dustball, perfidious chamber-pot,
Do you mean to imply that....

LYSE: Go there, see for yourself, Isabelle and Clindor
are....

MATAMORE: Poodle, cease your yap!
Trullish chambermaid, do you think
That such a gross Leviathan as myself would stoop
To spy upon my future queen,
The soon-to-be-empress of my limitless realms
In some seedy grape arbor with my little minion,

Thinking to catch them at illicit palaverings?
It is grotesque! It is vile!
It is loathsome!
Where's the arbor?

LYSE: Down this path.

MATAMORE: I knew that already. I am there.
Thus saying thus, swept the offended Matamore away.
(He exits.)

LYSE: The tender scene he'll interrupt
Is better torn asunder by this poltroon
Than by poor, love-torn, and dangerous Adraste.
There still is time—
I pray that madness travels faster
Than the spirit of revenge. *(She exits.)*

(Change of scene: in the arbor. CLINDOR *and* ISABELLE
enter.)

ISABELLE: My father's turned to stone,
A monolith on which is carved
The awful words: Adraste and Isabelle will wed.
He'd rather see me dead than married to a serving man.
It's not safe for you in this tyrant's house;
At any strange noise, we have to run.

CLINDOR: I can protect myself.

ISABELLE: Since we last met you've become as
irreplaceable
As the blood in my veins, as the air I breathe,
As my dreams at night, as my memory of joy.
Protecting you, I keep myself alive.

CLINDOR: My father's house is barred to me.
I have nothing to offer you, except....

ISABELLE: Except your love, which is all I desire.
The wanderings of the heart will at last find rest,
The vagaries of love will cease,

Here, here will be home forever,
For you, for me...my only, only love.

(Leaping from hiding place, MATAMORE *enters.)*

MATAMORE: Let Jove in heaven with thunderbolt split
This usurperous dog, this treacherous equerry!
I... *(He faints.)*

ISABELLE: Oh, God! Is he dead?

CLINDOR: No, not dead, merely
Overcome by prolixity.
Let me talk to him.

MATAMORE: Unspeakable machiavel!
False-foreswearing Judas-lips!
Et tu, Delamont?

CLINDOR: Thunder more softly.
I beg you, dread Goliath....

MATAMORE: I have no need to shout.
You know what you have done.
A crime so ghastly I cannot bear to pronounce it.

CLINDOR: I have stolen Isabelle.

MATAMORE: Precisely. You have two choices:
One: to be seized by the heels and flung
Straight through the celestial crystalline spheres
Into an abyss where the elemental fire will consume
What parts of you remain unripped by broken crystal.

CLINDOR: Sounds bad.

MATAMORE: It is. Or Two:
To be transformed by a spell I know
Into that lowliest of creatures, the naked mole rat,
Thereafter to be stepped on by my puissant boot
After which your skin will be made into a little
Ratskin purse for Isabelle to wear,
Embroidered with the words:
Thus died Delamont, traitor to his lord.

CLINDOR: Actually, there's a third choice.

MATAMORE: There is?

CLINDOR: Yes. I could beat you to a bloody pulp.

MATAMORE: I see. And which of the three will you choose?

CLINDOR: Guess.

MATAMORE: Look, you've obviously learned
A great deal from me. The ignominious deaths
I've mentioned ill-befit so well-trained
A soldier as yourself. Say you're sorry,
Promise to abjure the sight of Isabelle forever,
And we part as friends. Do you prefer that?

CLINDOR: I'd prefer to throw you in the river.

MATAMORE: I can't swim.

CLINDOR: That's too bad.

MATAMORE: Your spirit is astonishing! My warrior heart
Cannot but thrill to hear so brave a boast!
Spoken like a soldier! I am magnanimously moved;
I give her to you
As one warrior, however greater, to another warrior,
However less. I have so many lovers, I can share.

ISABELLE: It breaks my heart to lose the chance
To be your concubine, but I take solace
In knowing how relieved
The Queen of Iceland will be.

MATAMORE: She will; her ice-bound beauty,
Great as it is, was never match, my Isabelle, for you.

ISABELLE: Pronounce on us, colossal Matamore,
Your blessing and your benediction,
A thing my father won't provide....

MATAMORE: Let me be your father, then, if that's
The role I'm meant to play.

Pledge each other your vows.
I stand, for once, as silent witness.

ISABELLE: And I, for once, obey you, Father,
And join my heart, Clindor, to yours.

CLINDOR: Confirm that vow by giving me....

(ADRASTE *and* LYSE *enter.* ADRASTE *has his sword drawn.*)

ADRASTE: Your hand on hers, slave, is profanation.
Your punishment, to lose that hand.

(ADRASTE *slices the air with his sword.* CLINDOR *pushes* ISABELLE *away. The others scatter.*)

CLINDOR: (*Pulling a dagger from his boot*)
Her name upon your lips is even greater profanation;
Your punishment, to speak no more.

(*They begin to fight in earnest.*)

PRIDAMANT: This isn't dangerous, is it, it looks dangerous....

ALCANDRE: I'll make it disappear if it upsets you.

PRIDAMANT: (*As they fence*) No, wait, let me... Oh! Look at that! Look at him go. It's wonderful! Thrust! Thrust! Thrust! Thrust! Parry, hah! I...oh, I must be careful not to get overexcited.... Wow! What technique he has, he fences like an aristocrat, elegant but not foppish, not affected, what a fighter he....

(CLINDOR *stabs* ADRASTE.)

ADRASTE: Isabelle!

PRIDAMANT: (*Horrified*) Oh. Oh. He's dead.

(ADRASTE *dies horribly.* CLINDOR *dips his hand in* ADRASTE'*s blood and tastes it, raises his hand to the sky. Blackout.*)

(*The lights restore.*)

PRIDAMANT: What's happened? Where's Clindor?

ALCANDRE: In prison, of course, where murderers go.

PRIDAMANT: He's not a murderer! I know the law!
Self-defense, he was attacked!

ALCANDRE: He killed a nobleman. He has no means.
No lawyer to defend him. It's gone badly for him,
I'm afraid. The penalty is death.

PRIDAMANT: You lied to me. You said it turned out
well. I feel...a dreadful little tingling in my heart.
My valerian drops...

ALCANDRE: My servant will get you some water.
Then he must go.

(The servant brings PRIDAMANT *a glass of water.)*

PRIDAMANT: Go where?

ALCANDRE: Across the threshhold to the other side.
From here to there. He's eager to go.

*(*THE AMANUENSIS *does something to indicate exactly the
opposite.)*

PRIDAMANT: He crosses over? He...dissolves, a cloud of
vapor, like them? Does it hurt?

ALCANDRE: It exacts its price, yes.

PRIDAMANT: Then why put him through it?

ALCANDRE: My visions are concocted through a violent
synthesis, a forced conflation of light and shadow,
matter and gossamer, blood and air. The magic's born
of this uneasy marriage; it costs, you see, it hurts, it's
dragged unwillingly from the darkest pools.... I need
his agony, I'm a chemist of emotions, his misery's my
catalyst, it fuels my work, I regret the pain the journey
causes him, I'm fond of him I suppose but...I have to
keep the work interesting for myself, don't I? You can't
imagine, I've seen so many illusions.... *(To* THE

AMANUENSIS) Get going. *(Incanting over* THE
AMANUENSIS) Abandon the preservative chill of this
cave, give yourself over to strange, pulsing warmth;
the flow of blood, the flood of time, immediate, urgent,
like bathing warm in a southern ocean, rocked by
currents of another life. All that pain, and thwarted
hope, rejected love, grief, disappointment, joy...

*(*THE AMANUENSIS *disappears.)*

ALCANDRE: The heart chases memory through the
cavern of dreams. It will take a moment for him to
cross the threshold. Smoke your pipe, rest your eyes,
examine the contents of your purse, or of your soul,
or... A moment. And then I think we can begin again.

END OF ACT ONE

ACT TWO

ALCANDRE: Set the scene, *mysterium mechanicum*!
The moon, a dead man's pale white eye
Glowers down on your son, doomed now to die....
The night of his destruction creeps towards daybreak,
Shot through with terror, and the whispering breeze
Hissing songs about death through the cemetery trees.
We must begin, begin, begin.

PRIDAMANT: Your spirits seem to lift as my son's
fortunes decline. It's perverse. And insulting.

ALCANDRE: Contradictions accrete, complexities
accumulate, I do love a twist, a succulent complication.
I feel positively elated—you can never tell, when you
start these things, how they'll go—say, for example,
that your son had died a day or two after you booted
him out, or say he'd married early, and settled young,
in some dull domicile—a dutiful lawyer, say, how flat,
how inelegant that would have been. But here we have
a boy who's a troubling enigma, here we have a girl
with a fierce, conquering heart, here we have a meddler
who's made a mistake—she comes to us now, all riven
with remorse....

(LYSE *appears.*)

PRIDAMANT: And so she should. She's the cause of this
grisly farrago; it's a law of nature I tried to teach him: If
you trifle with women you set their tongues waggling;
but my son couldn't be taught, and here we are.

LYSE: It's a guilty murderer's moon that's rising tonight,
Spreading shadows over graves....
Tomorrow, at dawn,
The murderer dies, my lover, her love—unless....
I have a secret to confess:
I can play, if I choose, Madam Liberty;
I can, if I want to, set Clindor free.
I know a way to rescue him from death, but
I can't find a way to make myself want to.
Love and hate race after each other,
'Round and 'round
Till not even Solomon could tell them apart;
Indistinct, dangerous, frayed with pain
They riot in my grey and gloomy heart.
Is there no healing for this raw wound,
No shelter from this unforgiving wind,
No release from this life of love and loss?
The night's gone pale with fear of morning,
The setting moon's all undecided—
And before it drops behind the treetops,
A lunatic comes to worship it.

(MATAMORE *enters, bedraggled, furtive.*)

LYSE: Pardon me, sir...

MATAMORE: *(Terrified)* Aaaahhhh!
The maid! Oh, please,
Abuse me not, dread Medusa of the linen closet,
Neither giggle nor sneer, oh, dour farouche!
Your laugh might make to marbleize
My much-tormented soul.

LYSE: I'm not in a laughing mood tonight.
What are you doing in Geronte's house,
This late, alone? Where have you been?

MATAMORE: Three days ago there was a ruckus;
someone died.
I...I've been in the attic ever since.

LYSE: In the attic! There are rats in the attic!

MATAMORE: Oh, I know, man-sized rats,
My strength from battling them
Is sorely taxed; I thought the house
Would start and wake at the sounds our battle made:
Their screams of rodent agony, my shouts of glory
As I waved my sword....

LYSE: The footman said he heard noises in the attic....

MATAMORE: It was I.

LYSE: He said it sounded like someone weeping.

MATAMORE: It must have been someone else.

LYSE: Who?

MATAMORE: The rats. They wept.

LYSE: Weeping rats?

MATAMORE: Weeping rats; a gruesome sight.

LYSE: You were so frightened by the murder of Adraste
You've spent four days in the attic? What did you eat?

MATAMORE: Kitchen scraps and garbage, stolen at night.
Hannibal, they say, when crossing the Alps,
Would eat the dung of his elephants. So, though it was hard
For a man like me to root in the trash heap for mouldy meat,
I knew I was in good company.
And I didn't retire to the attic for fear,
But rather as a place of reflection. I needed time to think.

LYSE: And in these four days, your belly full of garbage,
What conclusions did you reach?

MATAMORE: That this life of love and violence is too much
For a man no longer young.

LYSE: It's wearing hard on everyone;
We're all suddenly growing old.

MATAMORE: But youth has its advantage still—
In these games of passionate exertion
My young apprentice, Delamont,
Has learned so well he far surpasses me.
I never killed a man.
I resign my place to him.
I plan to become a desert monk, a hermit in a cave.

LYSE: There are no deserts in France.

MATAMORE: I thought the moon.

LYSE: The moon?

MATAMORE: Yes, that moon, there.
I've given up hope for this cannibal world;
No good will come of it, or of its creatures,
But ah! the moon....
It's cold and bleak, they say;
Perhaps in a cave, on a comfortable rock,
Viewing the expanse of some lifeless lunar desert,
I'll learn to dream smaller, less tumultuous dreams.

LYSE: If you do learn, come back
And give me instruction....

MATAMORE: I can't, mop-and-bucket;
I'm not coming back. But think of me up there,
My peaceable catechism, draw patient forebearance
From that silvery light.

LYSE: I saw a moon-map once; there's a sea
I remember called Tranquility....

MATAMORE: Yes, yes, I'll find that sea,
Where respite's granted every wanderer
Weary of war, sick of desire....
I'll drink a cup of its water for you.
Adieu, adieu, remember me... *(He exits.)*

LYSE: More than remember: I'll worship you,
My patron saint; you catechize me:
To withdraw my poor heart from the lion's den,
To leave the blood sport of love to my betters.
Want, yes; but want less.
I see a way to a golden means,
By which I am revenged but nobody dies....
I have preparations to make
For an earthbound journey. And yet I will rise
Sky-high, even higher
Than if I followed this man to the moon. *(Exits)*

PRIDAMANT: Narrow the vision, this isn't what I've paid
for, you digress and I want to see Clindor, find out how
he's doing—I've visited prisons often enough, they're
terrible places, he's probably wretched. Show me that.

*(ISABELLE appears, kneeling. Behind her, THE
AMANUENSIS, dressed as GERONTE.)*

PRIDAMANT: No, no, not the girl, I...

ALCANDRE: Soon, your son, but
First this:
A handsome young woman,
At twilight prayers,
Watched over by her father—

PRIDAMANT: Her father! At last, the father arrives. And
now her entreaties will move him to free poor Clindor,
and he'll bring it all to a pleasant resolution.

(The hawk's cry is heard again.)

ALCANDRE: Beyond the window, a hawk, as it flies,
Traces in the skies
The jagged edges
Of her broken heart.

ISABELLE: Father, hear me...

GERONTE: Get off your knees.

ISABELLE: If you'll listen, I'll rise.

GERONTE: I cannot hear. I'm deaf as a stone.

ISABELLE: When I was a child, and sick,
My mother used to keep vigil by my bed
All night long.

GERONTE: Yes she did, I remember that. I resented you
for it,
Her preoccupation. You always were a troublesome
child.

ISABELLE: I'm keeping a vigil
For his deliverance; hear my prayer....

GERONTE: It's very odd; you look like me;
There's a distinct family resemblance, and yet
I can't seem to place you. At times you call to mind
A daughter I once had, sprung from the same
Flinty soil as I, made of fine, tight-woven stuff—
The goblins, I think, stole her away one wild night
And left a changeling in her place, a simpering,
Weeping girl, who throws herself at serving-men,
Whose tears are selective, reserved for paupers,
For little ragtag orphan boys....
But she's got no grief to spare, oh no,
For the grotesque murder of a noble young man
Who loved her dearly,
For whose destruction she is not, I'm ashamed to say,
Entirely free of guilt.

ISABELLE: Punish me, then, let me die in Clindor's place.

GERONTE: Oh, you'd like that. Whore and martyr, now
there's distinction.

ISABELLE: I am your daughter; if you love me at all....

GERONTE: Love, love, what does love mean?
Nothing! Anything can be called love,
Any ugly emotion—Love, that illusion,

That hydra-headed gargoyle into whose foul maw
Everyone tumbles, giddily, each
With the same insipid look
Of sheeplike expectation.
Love, that sarcophagus,
Love, that disease,
That demonic, black misery,
That catastrophe, love—do I love you?
Oh, yes. My daughter. Oh, yes I do,
But not like your pauper does, tender and moist,
Not with sweet, wet kisses
Tasting faintly of decay....
I love you, Isabelle,
With a heart of ice, drained and dry,
Bred of denial, restraint, and control,
A love whose flesh has been boiled off —
A clean cold hard white bonelike love.
I am the law. Come shiver in my arms.
No? You prefer, of course, your paramour,
His lawless extravagance, his oily heat.

ISABELLE: I'll show you, Father,
How true a daughter of yours I am;
I will become a deadly adversary;
A coiled viper as venomous as you.
I'll give you a hundred hidden reasons to fear me....

GERONTE: Be careful how you threaten:
My patience has its limits.

ISABELLE: Your worst threats hold no terror;
I'd rather you cut my throat
Than kiss my forehead, rather feel
The point of your knife
Than the touch of your hand.

GERONTE: Ludicrous bravado and wasted breath—
Here, my pampered patricide, here:
(*He throws his dagger at her feet.*)
Murder your father, astonish him,

Show him he was wrong to think you
Feckless, inconstant, weak-willed, and flighty....
(He waits for ISABELLE *to pick up the knife.)*
Before his blood's dried on the chopping-block, Isabelle,
You'll have found someone new to amuse yourself....

ISABELLE: Father. Hear me, hear what I pray.
Tomorrow when my lover dies
The world will see your hate triumphant,
A victory of arrant hatred, rank, and wealth,
Of sterile men and faceless law;
I congratulate you for this.
But, Father, please know,
The arm that raises the axe tomorrow
Is your arm; the neck on which it falls—
Not Clindor's neck, but mine.
When Clindor dies, I die.
In Paradise we'll be together;
And if you ever loved me,
And my dying brings you grief,
Know, Father, that I mock your sorrow,
That your tears and anguish will bring me
Joy. While you still live, the ghost of me will breathe
An icy cemetery wind through your bones every day,
And in the dark you'll hear me walking about, looking
for you.
Every day and every night;
You'll weep with relief when your last day dawns,
And till you die, I promise, you will envy me my death.

GERONTE: So be it. My daughter. My only child.
His sentence holds. It is the law. When the sun appears,
He dies. *(Exits)*

PRIDAMANT: It's abominable, isn't it, the way some
people treat their children?

LYSE: *(Entering)* What are you doing there
Down on your knees?

For a mad mad moment I thought,
"My God, she's scrubbing the floor!"

ISABELLE: Help me, Lyse.
I can't bear to live
A single instant after he is dead.
(She picks up the dagger.)
Look. It's my father's knife.

LYSE: Put it away.
There's a less painful solution.

ISABELLE: There's no other remedy.
Assist me or else
Become my enemy.

LYSE: I've saved him.

ISABELLE: Clindor?

LYSE: At liberty tonight.

ISABELLE: Tell me what to do.

LYSE: Meet me at the prison at midnight exactly.
I have the key to Clindor's cell.

ISABELLE: Lyse! How did you get it?

LYSE: His jailer is a lonely man.

ISABELLE: This sacrifice...

LYSE: Is even more than you imagine.

ISABELLE: I swear to you, if he goes free,
You'll live your days a wealthy woman.
I will wait on you.

LYSE: It's not your servitude I crave.
A handsome payment is another matter.
Here are the keys to your father's vaults;
Go in, pack a bag
With all the coins and jewels you can carry.

We flee tonight; you with your love, no longer lonely;
I with the loot, no longer poor.

ISABELLE: I'll give you half of all I have.

LYSE: Only half?

ISABELLE: It's a lot of money.

LYSE: You haven't seen the jailer.

ISABELLE: All then; everything.
You shall have diamonds for setting him free!
Clindor and I will need no gold!
I'll be his equal, we'll both be orphans,
Homeless and poor in the wide, wide world!
How happy we'll be!

LYSE: Both poor. I know Clindor will be overjoyed.

ISABELLE: It's you who deserve this ecstasy, not I.
I am your friend, Lyse, till the day I die. *(Exit)*

LYSE: Tonight when we open the door to his cell
He can claim his newly paupered bride;
I'll have a countinghouse consolation.
I wish them every penniless joy —
I'll jingle money at their wedding.
And how the hungry cat will cry
To find the fattest bird flown away.
Moderation is best, Aristotle said it:
Everyone feasts, but no one is full. *(Exits)*

PRIDAMANT: Well, if the maid is rich, my son's a fool
not to choose her—the other one's a bit high-strung,
and likely to be a spendthrift. On the other hand, the
maid's too scheming, it'd be constant work keeping up
with her. I only hope he doesn't make a mistake....

(ISABELLE and LYSE enter the prison.)

PRIDAMANT: Ah! The prison.

CLINDOR: I'm thinking of my father.
When they toss my trunk in the lime pit,
And my astonished severed head in after it,
Will you, father, in your house,
Oblivious, half-a-world away,
Feel some correspondent shiver in your spine?
When the sun and lime have bleached my bones,
Will your mouth, unexpectedly, inexplicably, go dry?
I am the orphan child of fate,
The hero of an old romance....
I think this is the end of me.
I can see the light grow green
And the night recede,
And the footsteps of the guards
As they arrive at my door;
I feel the irons on my wrists and feet,
The weakness in my legs
As we walk down corridors of stone,
The chill of the early morning in the walled courtyard,
The audience at attention, men my father's age,
The hooded stranger with the hand on the handle of the
axe
And then....

PRIDAMANT: No...

CLINDOR: My fear's so great I think that I've already
died,
And then I wake up, to rehearse it all again.
Why, in the depths of this open-eyed nightmare
Do I cling to a vision of you, Isabelle?
As though you can save me, by returning my love,
As though, wrapped in your love, I can't be killed.
I love you, Isabelle.
I really think that's true....
Oh, pardon, spare, forgive, relent,
I don't want to die.

(ISABELLE *and* LYSE *enter.*)

ISABELLE: God should not forgive you, my breath, my soul,
But beg your pardon for His villainy.

CLINDOR: This must be some illusion, some tantalizing dream,
Or else some early torment sent
To souls already damned....

LYSE: Not devils, sir, but
Angels of deliverance, flapping iridescent wings
And rattling keys.

(She opens the door to the cell. ISABELLE *runs to his arms.)*

ISABELLE: One more day apart from you and I'd have died;
With this embrace we're both restored to life.

CLINDOR: I'm not going to die?

LYSE: Eventually you will, but
Not for years and years.

ISABELLE: When death comes for you, Clindor,
As Lyse is right to say it will,
We two will have grown old and gray together,
Faithful through life, through death,
And till eternity ends.

LYSE: Yes, and there's no end to eternity,
Or to Clindor's capacity for love.
Come, before the dawn
Wakes your father from his dreams of execution,
We three must ride
Far beyond the reach of his law and his rage
To a freer, happier, more gentle land....
As we descend on our subterranean voyage,
I'll tell you a tale of the man in the moon....

ISABELLE: Oh, yes, Lyse, a story,
A story of love...

LYSE: A story of love...
Very well,
Once there was an orphan;
His father had banished him;
He was very poor;
His lover was wealthy, and she had a maid.

ISABELLE: And through a strange twist of fortune,
The ladies changed places,
And the poor, poor orphan married the one with no
money....

LYSE: And the poor, poor maid became very, very rich....

*(As they exit, LYSE removes her cloak; she is dressed
beautifully. ISABELLE opens her cloak; she is dressed plainly.
They laugh, hold hands, and face CLINDOR, who is first
bewildered, then dismayed; then he goes to ISABELLE and
kisses her. CLINDOR and ISABELLE exit. LYSE is stunned and
then runs after them as she hears the voice of GERONTE.)*

GERONTE: Come back! Come back! I banish you forever!
Forver! Forever! Return to me! My gold!
My child! My gold! My child! My gold!
Mine! Mine! All mine! All mine!

(The scene fades to black.)

PRIDAMANT: Thank God that's over. I can breathe again.
Light? Hello?

*(Again, the light on THE AMANUENSIS, who is ticking and
tocking.)*

PRIDAMANT: Yes, yes, I know, time's passing. No need
for the reminder. *(Recognizes him)* Ah! It was you! Her
father, heartless old Geronte, it was you! That was
amazing, you...incarnated him, you did, I've known
tight old bastards just like that, I found myself
despising you.... Tell me about it, crossing over.
Is it as bad as the old charlatan says it is?

AMANUENSIS: It's worse. He doesn't know. He's never been.

PRIDAMANT: He said he had.

AMANUENSIS: He lies.

PRIDAMANT: I thought as much. If you want to get the dirt on someone, make small talk with their servants. You probably never had your tongue cut out or your eardrums pierced, either....

AMANUENSIS: *(Hissing, furious, and very fast, as though pursued)* I did! I do! With a heated razor and bronze needles. You can't imagine what a fiend he really is. How I have to throw myself, again and again when he orders me to, into other lives, full of pain and twisted passion, how many demons are handed me in little bottles with the order, "Swallow this and be possessed!" While baby-fat men like you sit watching, devouring like pigs the agony I produce! Leech men, vampires, you smile, you're sated, you think blood won't call for blood, the crimes you commit are all shellacked, clean, and beautiful, while your refuse and sewage runs through me like a.... *(He stops in midsentence; his tongue is gone. He puts his hands over his ears; they're deaf.)*

ALCANDRE: Has my servant been amusing? What did he say to you?

PRIDAMANT: I've no idea. He seemed upset about something.

ALCANDRE: Ah, well, he usually is—it's this back-and-forth business, it wears on the nerves. The last vision is ready.

PRIDAMANT: Proceed. The married life of Clindor my son, and Isabelle his wife. I wonder if I have grandchildren.

(HIPPOLYTA *and* CLARINA *appear.*)

CLARINA: This is an endless walk, Hippolyta. It's taken half the day.

HIPPOLYTA: I need the exercise and air, Clarina; this grove is
A popular place. There's the Palace of Prince Florilame....

PRIDAMANT: I see they've changed the names again. This time I won't let it upset me. It's pleasant to see they've become friends. I had a maid once came into some money; she packed and left without so much as a thank-you-goodbye.

CLARINA: The Prince is away, at sea.

HIPPOLYTA: He's at sea and so am I.
While he's off with his cargo and his ships,
My equally enterprising spouse has been plying
The Prince's wife with merchandise of his own,
Offering her his inimitable protestations of love,
Which she buys wholesale, eager customer that she is.
This forest is their trading post;
They meet here every day and barter.
I'll walk until that merchant of adultery comes
And then...we'll haggle over prices.
Now you know why I'm here. Keep silent.

CLARINA: I can't. It's you who should keep silent.
Do you think your anger will alter him?
He's had a dozen affairs, and he'll have more,
The more you show him how you're hurt
The more he'll seek them out.

HIPPOLYTA: No, that can't be true.
There must be at least some little soul in him,
Some kernel of human shame he hasn't killed.

CLARINA: I think there was once. He got older.
None of the changes have been for the better.

There's a gradual wearing-down of things.
Accept it. Spare yourself this humiliation.

HIPPOLYTA: Humiliation's all I have, Clarina. I revel in
it.

CLARINA: You do. The two of you quarrel until you're
both hoarse;
You may not have a life together, but this dragon duet
Is only a way of driving each other mad.

HIPPOLYTA: We'll both rave, then. At least I won't be
alone.

CLARINA: Well, here he comes to keep you company.

HIPPOLYTA: Does he see me? He does. I can't....
Talk to him, please, tell him...

CLARINA: No, this game's best played, I think,
By two, not three, a thing I realized
Years ago. I leave you to your torture;
I've lost my appetite for injury
Through watching how you mull it over.
I'd rather live alone, and so should you,
But you, my poor, poor friend,
Like a beggar, linger outside the almshouse,
Waiting for either a kick or a coin.
Long ago this orphan lost his charm for me,
And I can't bear to watch the way
You beg for the wounds he inflicts.

(CLARINA and HIPPOLYTA run upstage to different corners.
THEOGENES enters.)

THEOGENES: Rosine, my own adored,
There's little time for pranks and teasing;
Our tryst today will have to be quick.
My wife's asleep, but she'll expect me home....

HIPPOLYTA: (Turning around) She knows where to
expect you, Theogenes.

And she's wide awake, though
She seems to be having a very bad dream.

THEOGENES: Oh, God...

HIPPOLYTA: In all the worst moments of your life
You make that little gesture and say
"Oh, God..." You are the filthiest liar
I've ever met; you can't possibly believe
That God would ever listen to you.

THEOGENES: You're mistaken, Hippolyta, I....

HIPPOLYTA: I was mistaken once; I remember the day,
Though you, I'm sure, don't.
You said you loved me.
I believed you.
I've become wiser,
And now I'm so rarely mistaken
I want to kill myself.
I gave up all the comforts of my father's house
To flee into poverty with you, a common soldier,
Incurred his wrath and broke his heart
And all for what? To stand here trading broken hearts
And tawdry lies with you? If you cannot love me,
Why did you abduct me? And if you will not love me,
And me alone, return me to my father. I'd rather bear
His gloating and contempt and live alone and without
love
Than drink this foul-tasting gall of yours.

THEOGENES: You know as well as I your father's doors
are barred,
You know his flinty heart won't melt,
Or else you'd have returned a hundred times before,
If your threats mean anything at all.
Go! Live on his doorstep! He may relent, although
If he's a whit like his child, he won't.
Like her he has no talent for forgiveness.

HIPPOLYTA: Forgiveness is for people who
Admit that they've transgressed.
How can I forgive you when you swear
You're guilty of nothing at all?

PRIDAMANT: Oh, this isn't at all how it should be!
They're wrangling like fish peddlers! Surely after all
they've been through they've become more elevated
and ennobled!

ALCANDRE: They seem instead to have gotten rather
tarnished in the process.

PRIDAMANT: Well, I don't like this dissolution. That first
vision was the best by far. I'll see if I can remember that
and forget the rest of it.

ALCANDRE: Considering what they'll cost, I can't
believe you won't try to retain them all....

PRIDAMANT: I came to you to launder the fabric of my
recollected life.
You haven't lived up to your promises.

ALCANDRE: I gave you back your son.

THEOGENES: And what have I done? Abducted you?
I abducted *you*? That's a lie; you know, Hippolyta,
You came willingly enough; your desire for me
Made you accomplice if not mastermind
Of your abduction; you're no victim.
I learned the art of murder for your sake,
And for your sake, I honed my skills
And built a bloody fortune up in service to the prince
To compensate you for your loss of wealth.

HIPPOLYTA: And the prince has amply rewarded your
bloody deeds,
And you, in gratitude, no doubt,
Have rendered service to his wife, and she,
Displaying the same fine fealty to the prince
As you her paramour have shown, accepts your

servitude;
Once a servant, always a servant; once false, then false
forever.

THEOGENES: Oh, that's exactly how you women think!
One mistake and everything's ruined,
One indiscretion means a thousand more;
Regardless of the uncountable kindnesses
Your husband may have shown,
The liberty, the veneration,
The indulgence of each weird request;
A husband may be Christlike in his sacrifice to you,
But catch him with a mistress....

HIPPOLYTA: Or two. Or three, or...
How many is it? I've lost count.

THEOGENES: And he becomes the Prince of Darkness in
your eyes.
Evil beyond all repair.

HIPPOLYTA: You're not the Prince of Darkness
Or the Son of God. Just something wearily in-between,
Hell-bent on disappointing. You keep me around
To forgive you your sins; with each indulgence
Fresh in your heart, you run out
To muddy your soul again
And then back again for more forgiveness.
I'm exhausted by this ritual:
I forgive you for everything, from now
Until the day you die, know that you're in a state
Of permanent absolution.
Forget about me, then, and my pardoning,
I'm tired of the subject of myself.
Think of the prince. Surely your benefactor deserves
Better from his favorite than this?
Are you completely lacking in simple gratitude?

THEOGENES: My treason to the prince embarrasses me,
but

To be honest, which I'm still capable of being,
In spite of your opinion that I'm not,
There's something in the danger and the treason
I find attractive.
If she weren't the prince's wife,
I wouldn't want the princess.
Don't forget
The circumstances under which
Our love first caught fire.
Didn't that tell you anything about my tastes?

HIPPOLYTA: I wasn't seeing as clearly then....

THEOGENES: You think that fire's dead.
It still burns furiously. Feel...

(He tries to put her hand on his heart.)

HIPPOLYTA: No... *(She touches it.)*
The heat's still there and still impressive;
It's just a trick you learned somewhere,
And meaningless.

THEOGENES: I love you. Allow me this betrayal.
You can find room for my insanity.

HIPPOLYTA: Clarina was right; I must enjoy
Being humiliated or I'd strike you now;
I only ask this: Consider the danger.
When the Prince learns what you've been doing,
What do you think will happen?
This isn't a game; it's treason, a crime.

THEOGENES: I know; death threatens me for this;
But I've spent my life in love,
And love is all I am; if I cease to love,
I cease to be; I dream of love; I eat love,
Breathe love, bathe my tired heart in love,
Pronounce love over and over and over again till
It sounds like a word from another language,
A word I've lost the meaning for.

How much do you think life really matters
To the creature I've become?
My only hope's that time will wear me out;
My flame will eat up all the air and die.

HIPPOLYTA: And when your flame's consumed the
atmosphere,
What will become of me, do you suppose?
When you've burned up and all the air is gone,
Do you imagine I'll live on, not breathing?
When we first loved our souls were joined
In joy and bitter struggle both;
We promised an exchange of hearts,
Forever, and, I think, try though you might,
One never does break free of that.
Our lives and deaths are married.
I don't ask you not to die,
But know that when you die,
I also die.

THEOGENES: You only think you will.

HIPPOLYTA: Oh, no. You'd understand, my love,
If, after all your talk of love,
You understood love at all.

THEOGENES: If our lives and deaths are bound together,
And if, in dying, I would cause your death,
It would also be the case, I suppose,
That you, in living, force me, your friend,
To live.

HIPPOLYTA: Careful logic, well constructed.
Your reasoning's impeccable.
If you could only promise me....

THEOGENES: I do.
I promise love forever, my single soul,
Complete, eternal, faithful....

HIPPOLYTA: If I could really have that,
For just one simple day,
From the morning till the evening,
Just once....

(THE PRINCE *enters.*)

THE PRINCE: Ah, Theogenes, there you are.

(HIPPOLYTA *and* THEOGENES *bow.*)

THEOGENES: Your Grace! Back sooner than you planned;
Did the weather turn your ship around?

THE PRINCE: A hurricane that blew up unexpectedly
From the Windward Islands;
And troubling news arrived from home.

HIPPOLYTA: I hope your wife, the Princess, is well.

THE PRINCE: Never better. The trouble's small,
A private matter, and easily dispensed with.
I've been hunting.

THEOGENES: I thought I heard your hawk.

THE PRINCE: Mmmm. You probably did. A pity.
This morning, at the hunt,
An archer killed him accidentally.
He served me very well, that hawk.

THEOGENES: That is a pity. Hawks are hard to train.

THE PRINCE: Yes, and rarely worth the trouble.
Too intelligent, too proud. The arrow
Caught him in mid-air; a perfectly constructed
Thing of flight, in an instant destroyed,
A tangle of broken feathers on the ground.

(THE PRINCE *suddenly draws a knife and stabs* THEOGENES
repeatedly.)

PRIDAMANT: No! Stop! Alcandre, stop this! He's being
murdered! That man is murdering my son!

HIPPOLYTA: *(Overlapping)* No! Please! Your Grace! Stop!
Clarina! Help! Murder! Murder!

PRIDAMANT: He isn't dead, he isn't dead....

CLARINA: *(Entering)* Oh, pity on my soul, Your Majesty,
what have you done?

THE PRINCE: Nothing that the law would not have done.
My wife, like my crown,
Are cornerstones in the edifice of state.
He should have known better.

HIPPOLYTA: Assassin.

PRIDAMANT: ASSASSIN! MURDERER! Alcandre, turn it
back, I...my heart...

THE PRINCE: Hippolyta, don't anger me.
Justice has been done for you as well;
He never was worthy of your love.

HIPPOLYTA: *(Falling)* I can't breathe,
Clarina, I'm suffocating.

(She collapses; the lights begin to fade.)

CLARINA: She's fainted. Help me.
Oh, God, she's cold, like him,
Already dead....

PRIDAMANT: NO! DON'T GO! THIS CANNOT BE! MY
SON!

*(A great red curtain falls. PRIDAMANT rushes toward it.
PRIDAMANT tears down the curtain. There's nothing behind
it.)*

PRIDAMANT: Gone... *(He puts his finger to the corner of
his eye.)* Look. What is this? *(His finger is wet.)* What's
happened to my eyes? Am I bleeding? No, it's clear,
not blood. Some kind of liquid. *(He eats the tear.)*
Mmmm. Salty, but quite delicious.

ALCANDRE: Ah. Good. Save a peck for me. *(He goes to* PRIDAMANT, *plucks a tear from his eye, holds it aloft between the thumb and forefinger.)* This, this jewel. This precious, leaded crystal pendant. This diamond Dolorosa, so hard fought for, so hard won, this food, my sustenance, for this infinitesimal seepage, for this atom of remorse, for this little globe, this microcosm in which loss, love, sorrow, consequence dwell in miniature, for this iota, this splintered particle of grief, for this I turn the gumstuck machinery, erect the rickety carpentry of my illusions. For this: to see your granite heart soften, just a bit.

PRIDAMANT: My heart, magician, doesn't soften, though under considerable duress, it breaks. Scar tissue forms. He's dead. His poor, unhappy wife. I'll join him soon. They could have dug a single grave for us both. I never dreamed I'd outlive him. Terrible day, to have seen that.... My eyes hurt, I want never to see again.

ALCANDRE: I have nothing more to show. It's over now.

PRIDAMANT: Finished, yes. It's over.

ALCANDRE: And I'm sure you're anxious to be on your way; at a steady gallop you might make Paris by morning.

PRIDAMANT: Paris? Why on earth would I go there?

ALCANDRE: To...see your son, of course.

PRIDAMANT: To see...? Is he buried in Paris, then?

ALCANDRE: Buried?

PRIDAMANT: I don't want to see his tomb; I hate boneyards, visiting the dead, wax flowers and weeping; it's a ghoulish custom.

ALCANDRE: There seems to be some...misunderstanding here, he's.... Oh, my.

PRIDAMANT: Yes?

ALCANDRE: Your son.

PRIDAMANT: What about him?

ALCANDRE: Well—

(Pause; ALCANDRE *looks to* THE AMANUENSIS *for help;* THE AMANUENSIS *only shrugs.)*

ALCANDRE: He isn't dead.

PRIDAMANT: He...I beg your pardon.

ALCANDRE: Your son's not dead, sir. Not really dead. I merely showed him to you in his present occupation, these...these scenes you watched are from a theatrical repertoire. Scenes from plays. Your son...

PRIDAMANT: Is alive?

ALCANDRE: Is an actor.

PRIDAMANT: Alive?

ALCANDRE: Oh, but yes, alive!

PRIDAMANT: Alive! Alive my son! Alive! I thought....

ALCANDRE: You didn't think this was real? Oh, I do apologize for that, sir, I do, I thought anyone could see.... Oh dear, oh dear, these mooncalves and mockturtles made of illusion and reality, they slip and they slither; I ought to be more careful, more punctilious; really, the distress you must have felt, it's inexcusable.

PRIDAMANT: Where? Where is he?

ALCANDRE: A charming little boulevard theater in Paris near the Tuilleries.

(He gestures to THE AMANUENSIS, *who gives* PRIDAMANT *a card with an address.)*

ALCANDRE: Twelve performances a week. Before I
sealed myself up in this hermitage, I was frequently in
attendance there. But that, ah well, that was years ago....

PRIDAMANT: *(Putting on coat, starting to exit)* I can go to
him, I can hold him again, kiss him and apologize, beg
forgiveness, I can leave behind this void, this cold and
haunted emptiness, and clutch him to me, warm and
strong and breathing and...breathing...he.... *(He stops in
his tracks.)* He's...an actor, you say. Tell me something.
That look I saw, the dangerous one—was that real,
or feigned, then?

ALCANDRE: Real or feigned? I've no idea.

PRIDAMANT: Then none of his life, this, none of it
real, not a fighter, an adventurer, not a pummeler of
aristocrats—none of that?

ALCANDRE: No.

PRIDAMANT: No. He's an actor. I don't know that I like
that. The theater—all that effort devoted to building a
make-believe world out of angel hair and fancy talk,
no more substantial than a soap bubble. You are moved
at the sight of a foul murder—then the murderer and
the murdered are holding hands, taking bows together.
It's sinister.

ALCANDRE: Oh, not so sinister. What in this world is
not evanescent? What in this world is real and not
seeming? Love, which seems the realest thing, is really
nothing at all; a simple grey rock is a thousand times
more tangible than love is; and the earth is such a rock,
and love only a breeze that dreams over its surface,
weightless and traceless; and yet love's more mineral,
more dense, more veined with gold and corrupted with
lead, more bitter and more weighty than the earth's
profoundest matter. Love is a sea of desire stretched
between shores — only the shores are real, but how
much more compelling is the sea. Love is the world's

infinite mutability; lies, hatred, murder even are all knit
up in it; it is the inevitable blossoming of its opposites,
a magnificent rose smelling faintly of blood. A dream
which makes the world seem...an illusion. The art of
illusion is the art of love, and the art of love is the
blood-red heart of the world. At times I think there's
nothing else. *(Little pause)* My servant has prepared the
bill.

PRIDAMANT: I pay bills promptly. I thank you for your
services.

ALCANDRE: We try to please our patrons, don't we,
my friend?

(THE AMANUENSIS *hands* PRIDAMANT *the bill, glaring at
him.)*

PRIDAMANT *(Looking at bill, then looking at card)* My son.
I remember the day he was born; I looked at him; this
small thing he was. I thought, "This is not like me.
This...will disappoint." And you see...I was right.
(Little pause) I may, if health permits, go to Paris this
spring, providing that they've put straw down on the
muddy roads and made them passable. It can swallow
you up, the mud. Still and all, it might be good to see
him again. My son, Theoge... No. His name started with
a "C". Crispin? Hmmm... All these memories, and I've
forgot his name. *(Exits)*

ALCANDRE: There were heavy rains this February and
March. I'd expect a lot of mud. Hah. I am...a tired old
fake. Well, goodnight, Dogsbody, make sure the lights
are out.

(ALCANDRE *vanishes.* THE AMANUENSIS *begins to lower
the lights. When they are suitably dim and theatrical,*
MATAMORE *enters.)*

MATAMORE: I want to leave this planet; don't like it
here!

Pardon, sir, can you tell me the way to the moon?
I'm lost and mapless, a wanderer through the world....

(THE AMANUENSIS *points. A huge white moon and stars
appear, floating in space.*)

MATAMORE: That way? You're certain of that? Yes,
The road that way seems to be going uphill. *(Exits)*

(THE AMANUENSIS *is alone. He puts a tentative finger in his
mouth. The tongue is back. He smiles.*)

AMANUENSIS: Not in this life, but in the next.

(He turns out the lights.)

END OF PLAY

CPSIA information can be obtained
at www.ICGtesting.com
Printed in the USA
FSOW04n1550090116
15369FS